LEA
TOGET
SCIE

WATER AND AIR 2

Richard Dawson

A Piccolo Original
Piccolo Books

Note to parents

Welcome to this book.

Science hides behind the mysterious veils of difficulty and incomprehension – brush aside these veils and it is fun!

This book, **Water and Air 2**, contains facts, puzzles and experiments put together to give children a fun start to the world of science.

The activities in the book are similar to the science activities your child will be engaged in at school and are firmly linked to the National Curriculum. Science is the practical activity of finding out, so your child may require some help with the reading of instructions before they are able to engage in the activity.

Whether you are reading, exploring or recording, join your child and enjoy the partnership of learning together about **Water and Air 2.**

Equipment list: jam jars, tubing (home brewing tubing is best, it's widely available and fairly cheap), yoghurt pots, funnel, empty tin, candle and balloons. All other equipment can be found around the house.

First published 1994 by Pan Macmillan Children's Books
a division of Pan Macmillan Publishers Limited
Cavaye Place, London SW10 9PG
and Basingstoke

IBSN 0 330 33038 X

9 8 7 6 5 4 3 2 1

A CIP catalogue record for this book is available from the British Library.

Typeset by Pan Macmillan Ltd
Printed and bound in Great Britain by
Henry Ling Ltd, The Dorset Press, Dorchester

Water, water, everywhere!

Get a potato . . . feel it.
How does it feel?

Now peel it!

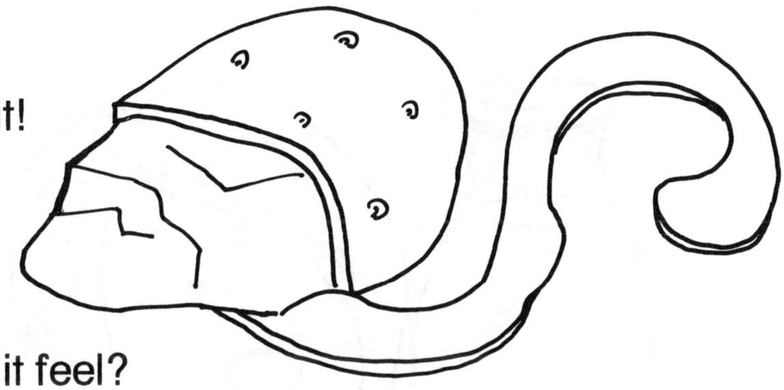

How does it feel?

Now chip it!

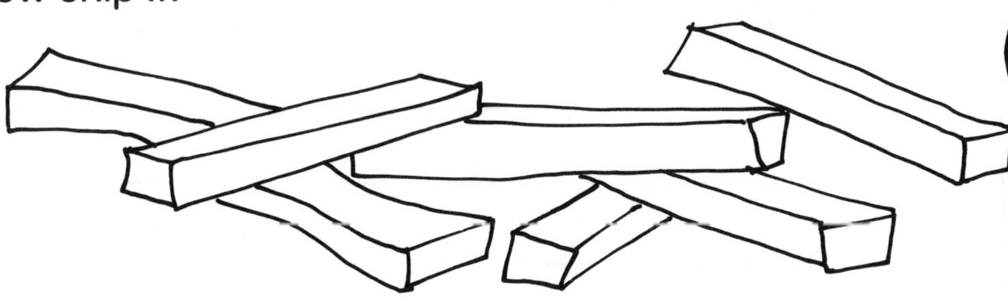

Feel each chip . . . where has all the water come from?

What do you think a potato is mostly made of?

Even in the air you breathe!

Get a bottle of milk from the fridge. It must be really cold.

Breathe on the bottle. Look at the cold glass. What can you see?

Where has it come from?

On the up . . .

Water can flow uphill!
Get a small strip of towelling material and two jars.

Put water in one jar and join the jars by the material.

Leave the jars overnight.
What do you notice next day?

____

____

How did this happen?

____

____

Over the top

You will need to be in the kitchen.

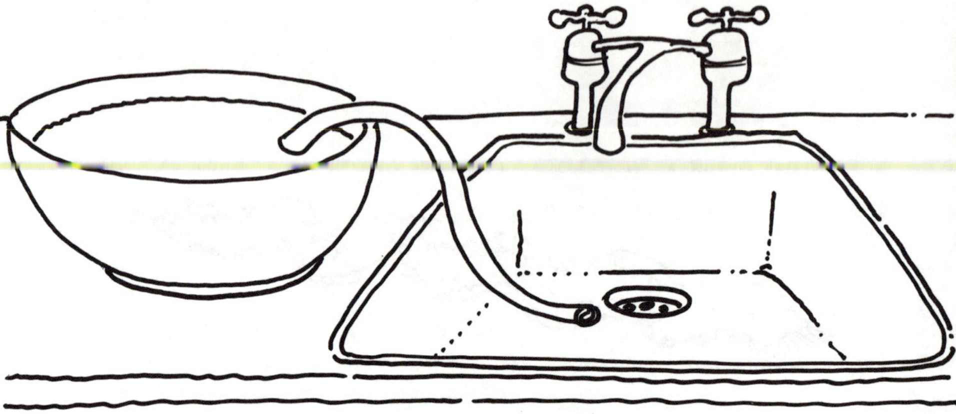

Get a bowl of clean water and a clean peice of tubing. Put one end of the tubing in the bowl and suck until the water reaches your mouth. Quickly take the tube out of your mouth and put it in the sink.
What happens to the water in the bowl?

We call this syphoning.
Any liquid can be syphoned – but some taste bad!
How can you stop the syphon?

Stop it . . .

You need a milk bottle and a sieve.

Fill the milk bottle full of water and put the sieve over the top of the milk bottle.

Tip the bottle upside down over the sink.

What happens?

Skin deep

Balance a needle on the prongs of a fork.

Carefully lower the fork into the water.
What happens to the needle?

Add one drop of washing-up liquid to the water surface. What happens?

Floating and sinking

Get a ball of Plasticine and drop it into
a bowl of water.
What happens?

Take out the Plasticine and shape it into a boat.

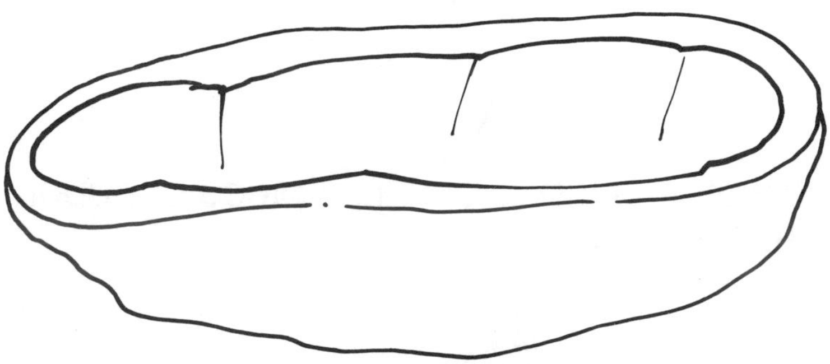

Float the new shape in the water.
What happens?

Water lily

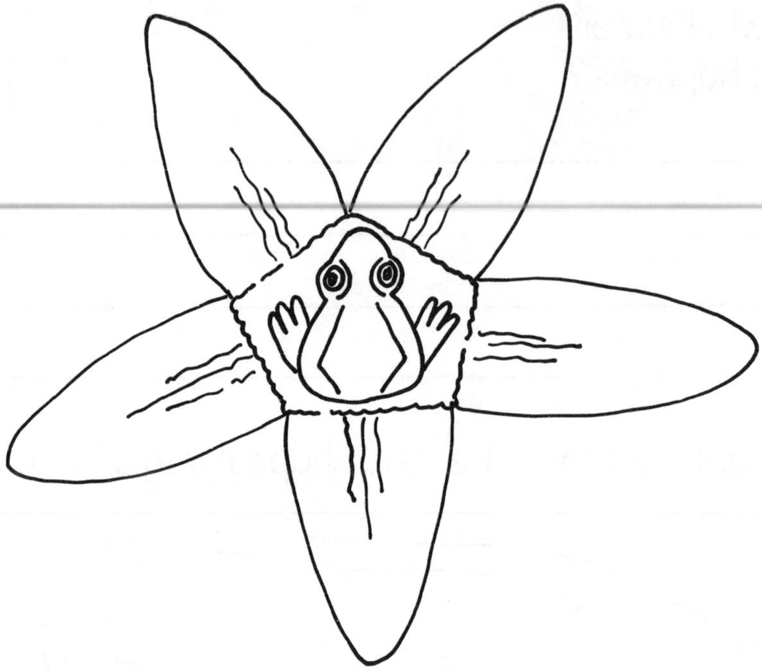

Trace the water lily on to a stiffish piece of paper.
Fold up the petals like this:

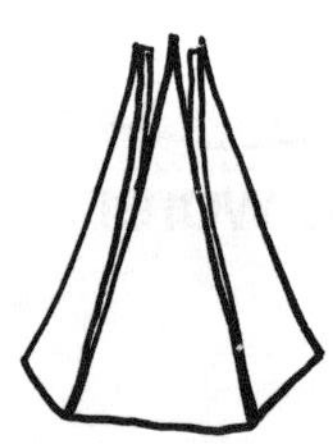

Now float it on a saucer of water.
What happens?

___

___

___

Floating penny

Put a penny on the bottom of a bowl. Fill the bowl a quarter full with water from a jug. Now stand where you can look over the brim of the bowl so that you can see the edge of the penny.
While looking at the penny, slowly pour more water into the bowl.
What appeared to happen?

Have you ever noticed your feet when you are standing in the swimming pool?

Sounds good

Bang two stones together.

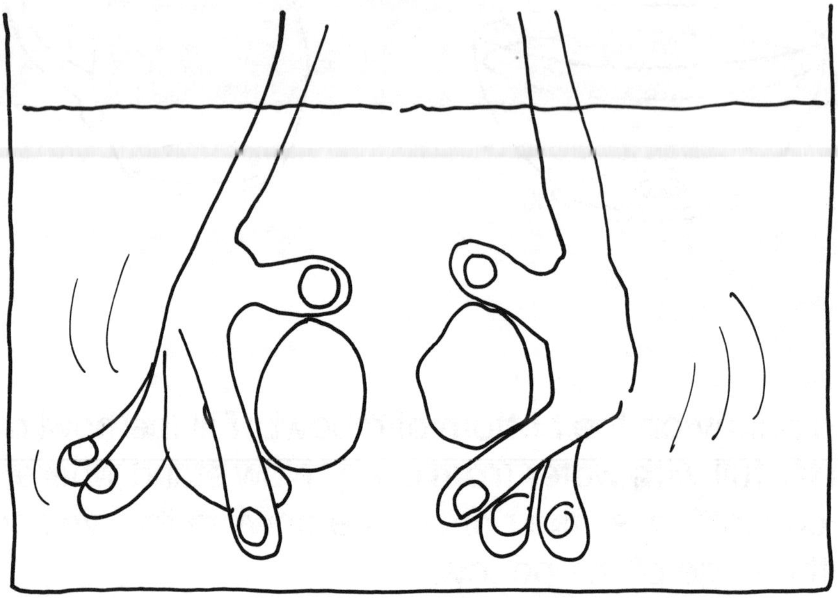

Now bang the stones together under water.
What do you notice about the sounds?

Have you ever noticed that sounds seem clearer on a foggy day than on clear days?

Clean up!

Make some dirty water!
Put some soil in a jar of water.

Cut a circle from newspaper. Make it into a cone and slip it into a funnel.

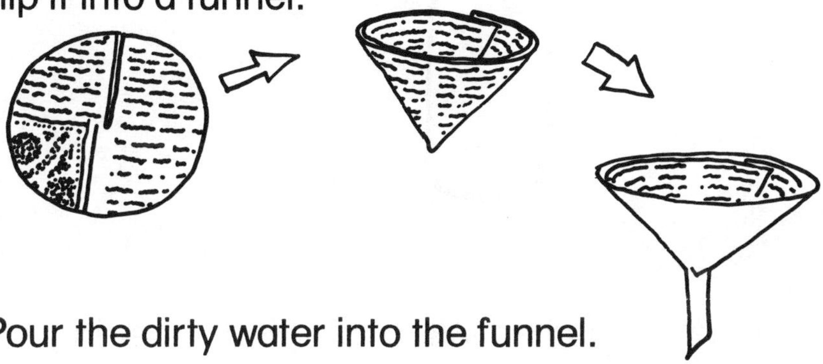

Pour the dirty water into the funnel.

What happens?

____

____

All the water you drink is filtered before it reaches your house!

Under pressure

Carefully balance an ice cube on the top of a milk bottle.

Tie two spoons together with a thin piece of string . . . and hang the spoons on the ice cube.

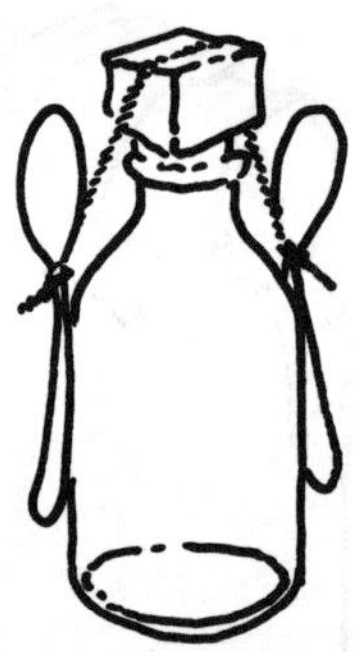

Carefully put the bottle, ice and spoons in the fridge and wait an hour. Now look at the ice cube.

What has happened?

____

Do you know why?

____

Time drips by . . .

Make a water clock. Make a small hole in the bottom of an empty tin.

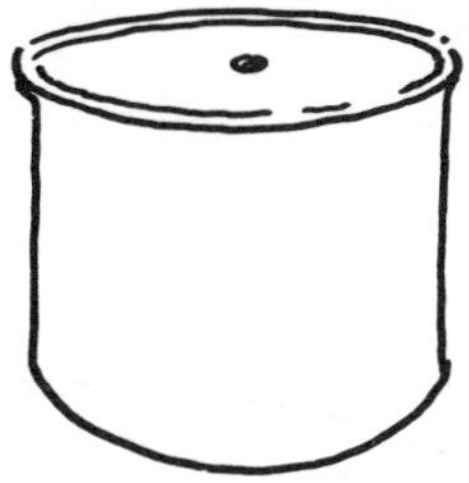

Fill the tin with water and stand the tin on top of a jar.

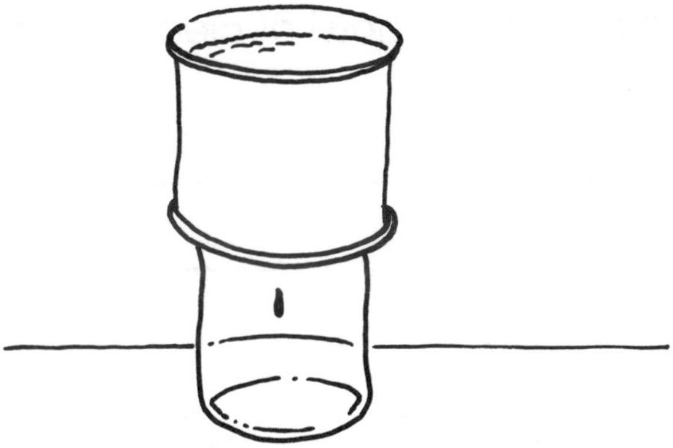

Use your watch and mark the level of water in the jar at five minute intervals, until the tin is empty.
What do you notice about the marks on the jar?

Refill the tin. Do the drips fit the marks you made?

Have you made a good clock/timer?

Soap power

Cut a little boat from card or balsa wood and make a small notch at the back.

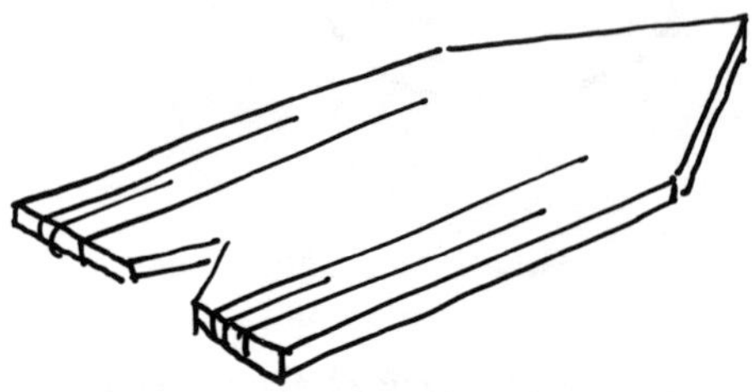

Float your little boat in a bowl of clean water. What happens?

____

____

Take the boat out of the water and push a small piece of soap into the notch. When the water in the bowl has settled put the boat with the soap back into the water. What happens?

____

____

All bottled up

Stuff a paper tissue in the bottom of a jar.

Turn the jar upside down and stick it in a bucket of water.

Remove the jar from the bucket.
What do you notice?

____

____

How did this happen?

____

Up and under

Get two jars and fill one with water. Put the two jars under water.

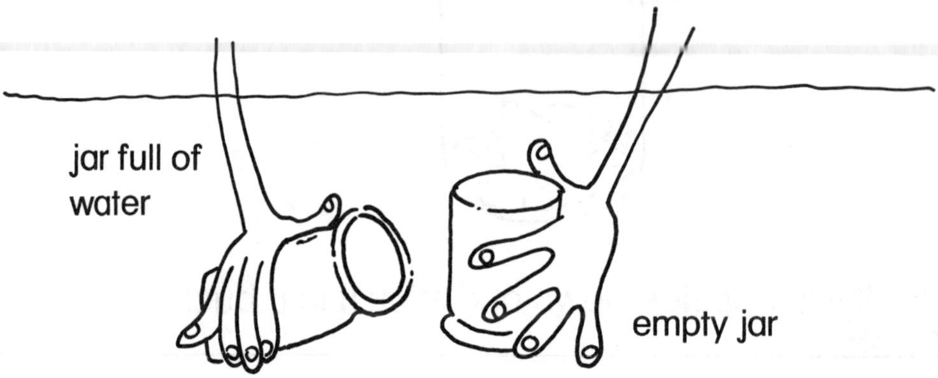

Bring the empty jar to the full jar.

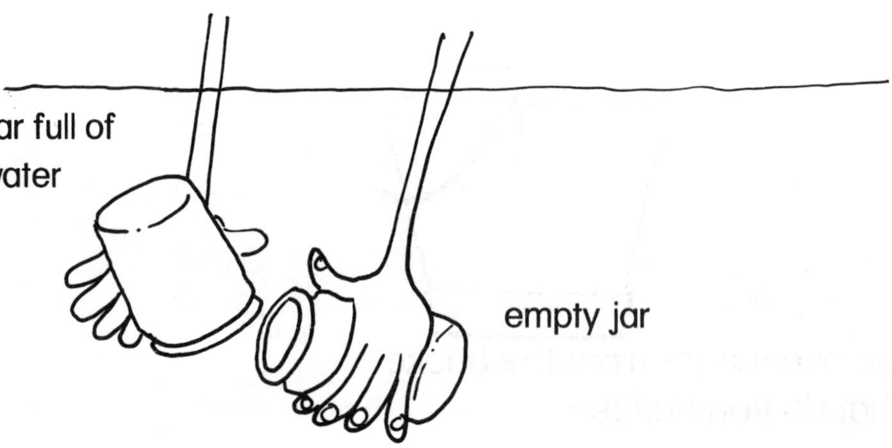

What happens?

____

____

The big drips

Mix some watery paint and drip it on to the circle from about 30 cm.

Drip some more paint from one metre.

How are the splash marks different?

It gets into everything

Find a stone or piece of brick. Drop it into a jar of water.

Draw what you see.

Going up!

Be very careful when you do this experiment. Make sure an adult is close by!

Put some water in a saucer and stand a candle in the water. Light the candle.

Put a jar over the candle.

What happens?

Why?

Full of air

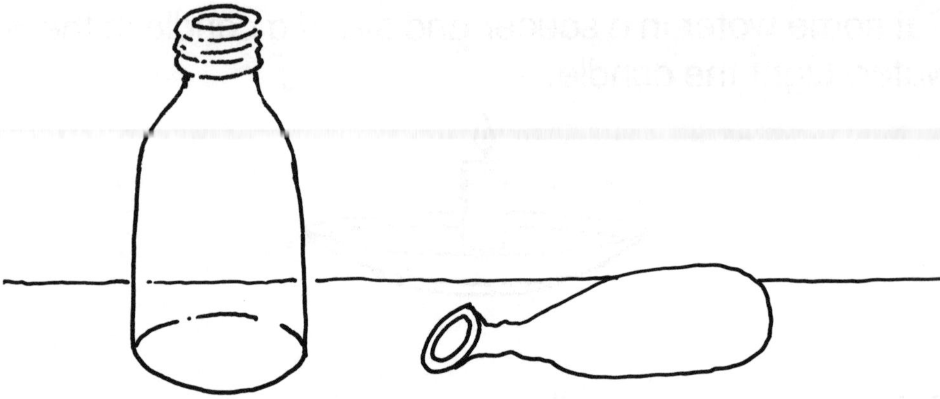

Get a small bottle and put a balloon over the neck.
Stand the bottle on a radiator.

What happens? ________________________________

____

____

Why? ________________________________

____

____

A quick blast

Hold two sheets of paper in front of you and blow in between the sheets.

What happens?

Blow away

Put a sheet of paper on two books. Blow along the table top and see how far you can blow the paper.

What happens? ______________________________

____

____

____

____

Air flow

This will take some doing . . .
Inflate a balloon and fasten it on to a piece of tubing.

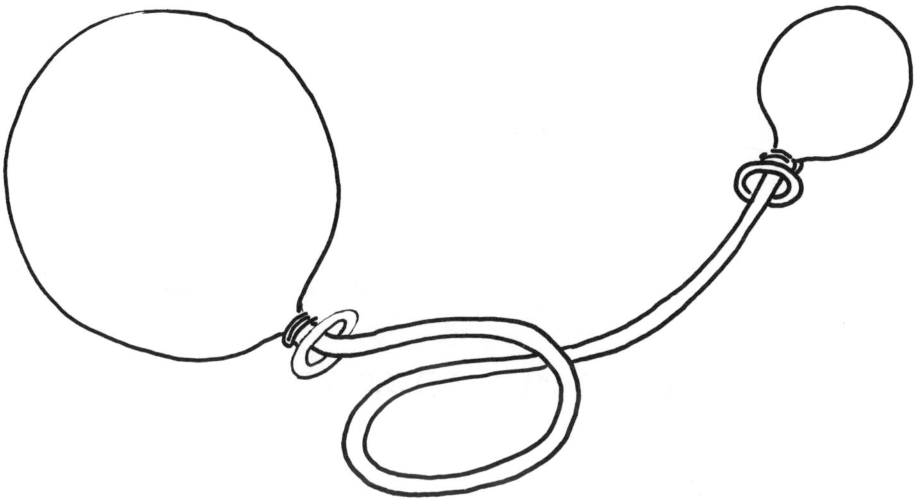

Fix a deflated balloon on the other end of the tubing.
Squeeze the inflated balloon.

What happens? ______________________________

____

____

____

____

Air lift

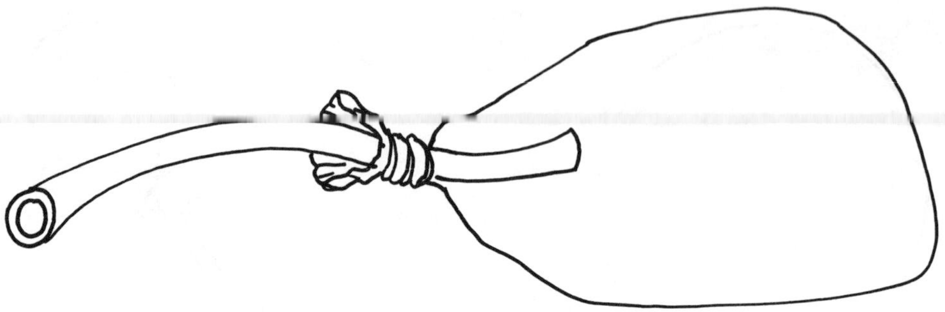

Tie a piece of tubing on to a plastic bag.

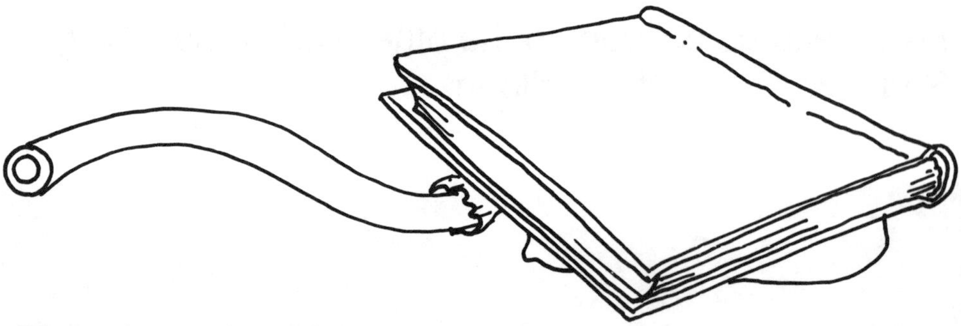

Blow down the tube.

What happens?

Heavy weight?

Make a simple balance from:

1. some string

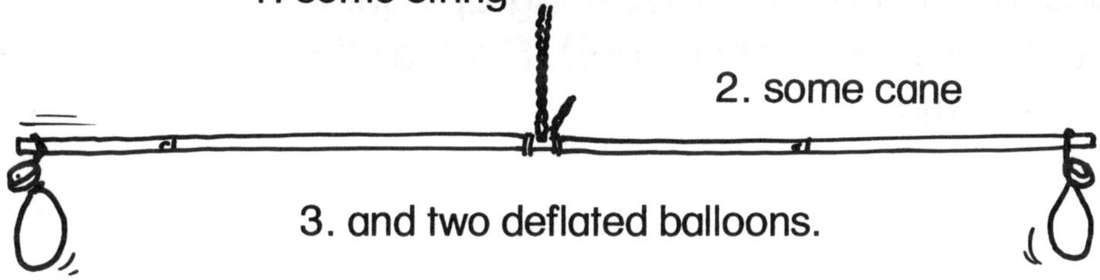

2. some cane

3. and two deflated balloons.

Remove one balloon. Blow it up and hang it back on your balance.

Draw what you see.

What do you think this means? ____________________

Under pressure

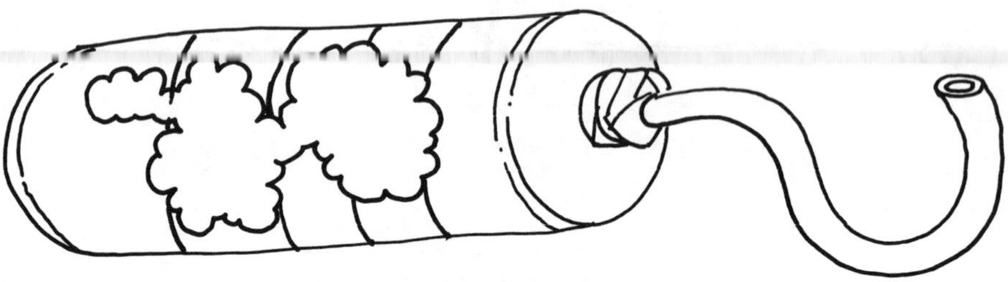

Fix a tube in an empty washing-up liquid bottle (make sure it's really clean!). Suck all the air out of the bottle.

What happens? ________________________________

Why? ________________________________

Jet propelled?

Blow up a balloon and then let it go . . .
See if you can draw the balloon's route!

Under and over – a crossword

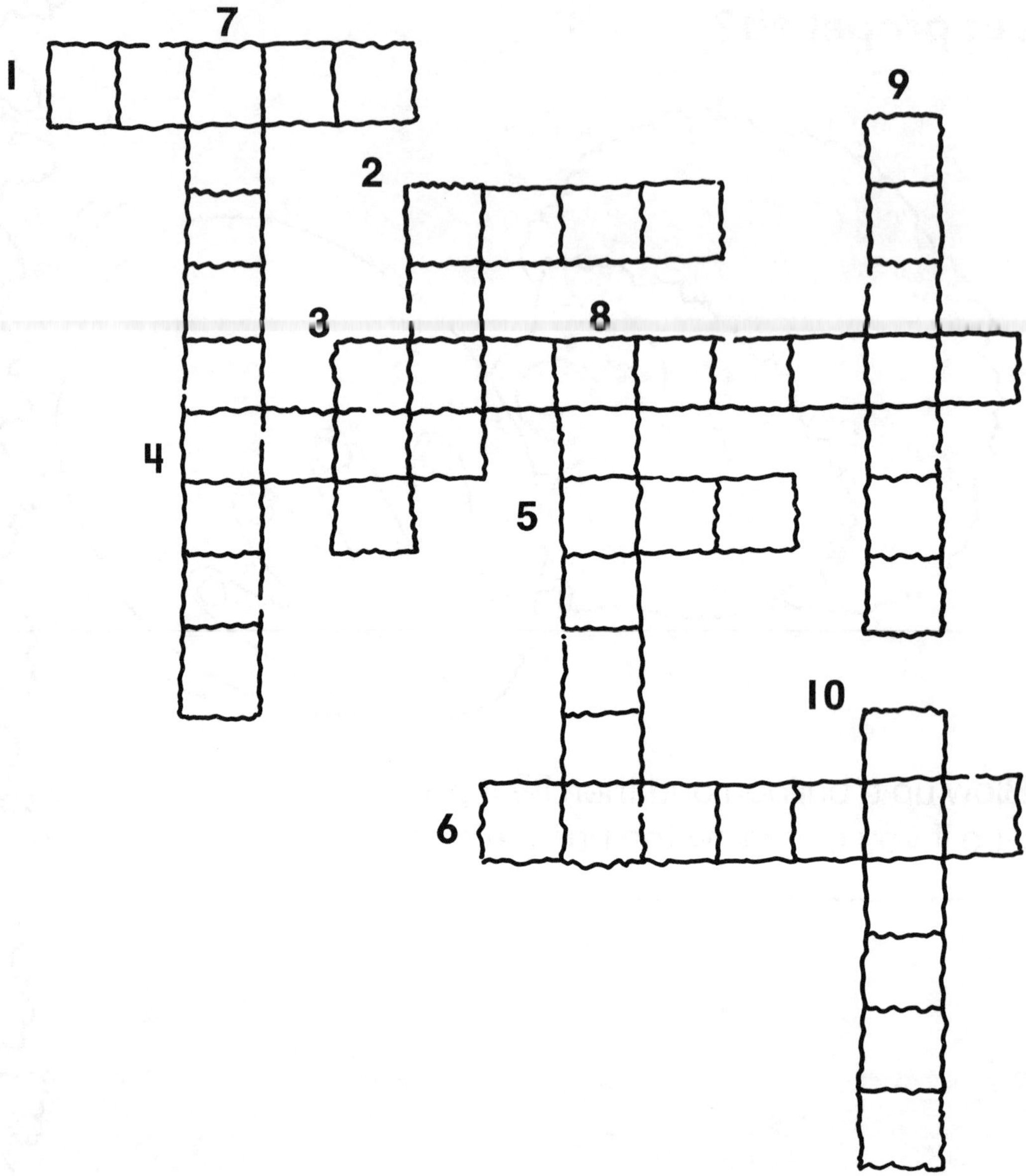

Across

1. Large sea creature
2. Side of a river
3. Underwater boat
4. Large area of still water
5. Oxygen, nitrogen, helium
6. White sea bird

Down

2. A sky colour
3. Above us
7. Sky vehicle
8. When birds fly south for winter they ________
9. Sky spectrum
10. Plane with no engine

Where does it go?

Mark with an **A** for air or **W** for water. Will some do both?

The answers

page 3	Water
page 4	Water vapour condenses from the breath.
page 5	By **capillary** action in the cloth. This is the movement in plants from one cell to the next cell, either upwards or downwards. This is how plants get water from the ground through their roots to the leaves at the top of the plant.
page 6	By lifting the sink end of the tube above the bowl end.
page 7	Most of the water stays in the bottle.
page 8	The needle sits on the surface **tension** of the water. When the surface tension is broken, the needle sinks. Surface tension is the 'skin' of the water.
page 9	The boat shape floats.
page 10	The 'flower' closes.
page 11	The light from your feet is 'bent' as it passes from the water into the air.
page 14	Pressure raises the melting point of ice.
page 16	The soap destroys surface tension and should cause the boat to move. See answer to p6 for **tension** explanation.
page 17	The air in the jar is compressed and does not allow water into the jar.
page 18	The air will rise out of the first jar and can be trapped in the second jar, forcing water out of the second jar.
page 20	Air bubbles should be seen rising from the stone.
page 21	The oxygen is used up in burning (one sixth of air is oxygen) and is replaced by the water.
page 22	Air expands when it is heated.
page 27	Air has weight.
page 28	The air pressure inside the bottle is reduced, and the external air pressure squashes the bottle.
page 30	Across 1. Whale 2. Bank 3. Submarine 4. Lake 5. Gas 6. Seagull Down. 2. Blue 3. Sky 7. Aeroplane 8. Migrate 9. Rainbow 10. Glider
page 31	Flying duck, Flying fish, Plane, Floating duck: A/W Hovercraft, Airship: A Submarine, Fish: W